LET BATTLE COMMENCE

Beat! beat! drums! – Blow! bugles! blow!
Walt Whitman 1861

Wendy Klein

Let Battle Commence

First Edition ISBN: 978-1-913329-14.3

Wendy Klein has asserted his authorship and given her permission to
Dempsey & Windle for these poems to be published here.

Front cover design © Hannah Starks

Published by Dempsey & Windle
15 Rosetrees
Guildford
Surrey
GU1 2HS
UK
01483 571164
dempseyandwindle.com

British Library Cataloguing-in-Publication Data
A catalogue record for this book is available from the British Library

Printed by CMP Ltd, Poole, Dorset, U.K.

Writing my great-grandfather

Just over five years ago, my cousin, the artist Ippy Patterson, sent me 175 pages of letters written by my great-grandfather, Robert Melvin Tarleton Jr, to his mother and to his fiancée, later his wife, Sallie Lightfoot while he was serving as a Confederate soldier.

Although I've never been much interested in genealogy, I was intrigued with this slave-owning gentleman who had the same name as my paternal grandfather and my own father. As I browsed through the many pages of typewritten text, painstakingly copied from the handwritten originals, I brooded over whether there might be some poems from them.

Little did I know how difficult it would be to extract them, to do justice to the many passionate, articulate letters written by my ancestor over that time period, whose beliefs could not have been more different from my own. It has been a slow process, with many setbacks, and I am grateful to my husband Stephen for listening to all my drafts and for encouraging me when I did not feel equal to the task.

Thanks are due to the patience of my workshop peers who had to critique the poems out of context; in particular: Gina Wilson, David Olsen and Sarah Watkinson. Deep thanks especially to Charles Lauder, former co-editor of *The Interpreter's House*, whose insight and knowledge of that period of history, plus keen editorial skills, have helped me to pull the piece together. And of course, enormous gratitude to my cousin Ippy for bringing the letters to my attention, supplying the images of Robert and Sallie and generally filling me in on bits of family history I had not previously known.

Let battle commence!

Wendy Klein
March 2020

Contents

Introducing Your Very Own Great War

The U.S. Civil War, also called the War Between the States, was
fought on American soil between 1861 and 1865. Death toll was not
equalled by the combined toll of other American conflicts until the
war in Vietnam.
(American Battlefield Trust)

EXTRA, EXTRA! Read all about it!
your very own great war
brought to you by Messrs. A. Lincoln
and J. Davis, made manifest
by Generals R.E. Lee and U.S. Grant
America's best and biggest war.

Introducing, for maximum effect:
ironclad ships, armoured to prevent
easy sinking, most useful
for long-range warfare.

Bringing you trench warfare, model
for the next great war, the Gatling gun --
worthy precursor to the machine gun,
as we know it.

Oh, and the very first landmines,
leading the way to Armageddons
everywhere, and last, but not least,

the Minie ball with its increased range
and accuracy, replacing the clunky old rifle,
so cumbersome, so slow to load.

How clever you've become at maiming
one another, at killing
what giant steps forward, your greatest war.

i. The Cause

*i.m. Lieutenant Robert Melvin Tarleton
(1838-1868), my great-grandfather*

Who cared
whether it was just or not?
The stories made your blood sing:
the grooved Minie ball
that a boy picked out
of a freshly ploughed row
and rolled in his palm
made him part of a moment
that happened over a century before.

My great-grandfather imprisoned
in my roll-top desk

*… they do not yet look upon us as a nation, firm and well balanced, and they will
never admit the superiority of the Southern soldier until the iron storm of war
shall burst upon their own cities and fields…*
Lt Robert Melvin Tarleton, August 18, 1861

Though he says nothing for or against slavery, he was
fighting for the wrong side, believing devoutly
in the rightness of the Confederate cause,

so I keep him here, along with a pile of mending,
a crocheted pin cushion, twenty spools of cotton
in assorted colours, the 175 pages of letters he wrote

while serving as a lieutenant in Smiths Battery, Kentucky.
This imprisonment is cosy, a holiday camp compared
to the Yankee gaol he will escape from to marry

my earnest young great-grandmother, Miss Sallie Lightfoot.
The letters give no clue to the smallpox, rubella – their wildfire
spread, killing hundreds -- the horror and despondency

that hardened veterans thought more heinous than the carnage
of bullets and grapeshot that tore ragged holes through
their advancing lines each day. When I walk past the desk

I touch its golden-oak finish, revealed after hours spent
sanding off its sombre Victorian stain, but I do not
lift the lid, do not disturb his papery slumber.

No, he will stay put until I am ready not to misrepresent him.
That he was clever and brave, I do not doubt,
but for now, I shan't let him out.

I Meet Him

in media res, muffled up to the chin
in confederate grey, double-breasted,

best wool worsted, what looks like
a pert bowtie under his stiff collar.

His dark hair is sleeked flat for the photo,
a patrician left ear exposed next to

a sideburn clipped short for the period.
His cheeks are clean-shaven

by a keen straight razor, sharpened
and wielded, no doubt, by his black valet.

I imagine his eyes are Tarleton-blue,
a clear sapphire like my father's,

his father's – grave and mischievous in turn.
It is early summer, and he's enlisted

on his first day back from med school,
proud to serve, certain he will be home

by Christmas. We've all seen Civil War photos,
black and white images of bearded Union generals

or moustachioed Confederate colonels,
posing to one side of the camera,

dead bodies spread out on the battlefield,
or common soldiers around a camp tent.

This photo is of a different order. It is
a memento, taken for a mother,

a sister, a future wife. It is a photo that says
I will return safe and sound;

we are strong, we will win. It is a vestige
of a former life. Let battle commence.

Lifting the Lid

i.m. Robert Melvin Tarleton

The desk has never been secured, its brass lock,
only an ornament for decades – the finger-holds

either side of the lid as smooth and responsive as ever,
the slats folding in on one another clack on clack

until the top is revealed. And yes, the folder is still there,
next to the stacks of half-perused books – my research

unfinished. I know he is under it: my great-grandfather,
abandoned months ago, after chasing his shadow

through history, through fiction, tracking his scent
between the pages of *Cold Mountain,* wondering whether,

like Inman, his heart was so touched by the fire
that he would never make a civilian again.

I believe I can almost smell him between the lines
in Bruce Catton's accessible history, that heart-rending

good sense about his war, the wretched misunderstanding;
neither side realising until it was too late, that the other side

was desperately in earnest. When the lid is lifted, I imagine
I hear his youthful voice, a full-throated Rebel yell.

Rebel Yell

18 August 1861, Norfolk Virginia

And in his first letter:

How I hate garrison duty. Of all things detestable
is the thought I will never see a Yankee,
though I hear their guns in the distance each day.

I think there should be a Manassas every week
until one side is whipped. Many of us believe
such a battle would bring the North to its senses.

They will not know until the iron storm of war
shall burst upon their own cities and fields!

I believe the war will never end while we remain
on the defensive; that the shortest way to end it
is the bloodiest kind of aggressive warfare.

Let us commend the poison chalice to their own lips;
let them realize what a horrible thing war is,
and perhaps they may consent to peace.

Manassas

War is a very slow thing after all. Pity we could not have a Manassas battle every week until one side was whipped.

Lt Robert M. Tarleton, August 18, 1861

Man aaaaaa ssas 1en 3 esses, the stress
on the second syllable, drawn out –
draaawn out even longer by his drawl,
for in my mind he drawls, a restrained
gentlemanly drawl.

MANASSAS: *The Civil War,* a history by Bruce Catton,
Battles of, see Bull Run
Bull Run, Va., First Battle of, July 21, 1861

The date, less than a month before this letter
to his mother – oh my young great-grandfather,
college boy, just down from university,
oh, your Confederate zeal. You complain
about the paucity of news, newspapers.
Curse or blessing?

EXTRA! EXTRA:

*Rebels launch a counterattack, union force
withdraws, the retreat turned into a 'rout'*

*Lieutenant General Thomas Jackson,
earns his nickname 'Stonewall'*

rout: Chambers Dictionary
noun   a defeated body
an utter defeat
disorderly retreat.

synonyms: defeat, retreat, conquest
overthrow, beating, trouncing, drubbing.

Union	Confederacy
18,000 engaged	18,000 engaged
460 killed	387 killed

Rout, or draw? Oh, you blue-eyed optimist,
my great-grandfather; statistics will not be
your strong suit.

Smith's Battery
Columbus, Ky.
Dec. 30th, 1861 – in his own hand.

This brave o'er hanging firmament

does very well in fine weather
but leaks very badly in wet,
Myself and mess have been
hard at work on it for two weeks,
and though not completed, it is now
habitable...

To us, not one of whom ever worked
before on the roof that was to shelter him,
it seems a very paragon of houses --
the furniture not elegant,
but substantial:

a couple of rude plank bedsteads
two or three benches
a crazy-looking campstool
a worn-out broom, two or three trunks
as many valises lying around loose,
a table – borrowed tonight
for a game of Euchre.

But the fireplace, ah the fireplace:
seven feet wide, it throws out heat
beautifully. The reason
for this long rigamarole
about a very ordinary log cabin
is that I have a warm place
to warm my fingers
so I can write to you.

What a piece of work is man...

P.S.

Winter is coming;
I don't know what we will do
to keep from freezing

send thick woollen shorts for later on
at least two in blue or red
or any durable colour

and two pairs of grandmother's knit
woollen socks -- Aunt Roxie to knit them.

Also thank you for the bottle of pickles
the one of claret, but broken,
the ham and peaches.

P.P.S.

You need not look for me in Mobile this winter
but know I am in excellent health
and very well pleased here; The duties
of a cannoneer are light and pleasant,
but if only I could see you all occasionally
hear the girls play and get a good dinner
I should be perfectly contented. Promise me
you will make the charming Miss Tarletons
and the fascinating Misses Dargen practise
their piano. If the war lasts very long
they may have to concertize for bread.

The Real Rebel Yell

It's not a yell, said an old man on Bayou Teche,
but a fox call, that strange warbling that rose
from the throats of thousands of boys and men

clad in sun-faded butternut and moss grey rags
when they charged through the smoke and dust
at the Union line, their boys and men

togged out in robust woollen blue. How did they find
that kind of courage? His sons could have heard
veterans try to imitate the sound.

But it wasn't just the sound: a series of *woos*
like an owl hooting that rose to a wolf-pack
in full-throat on the heels of its prey,

the vowel both rounded and restrained, a howl
pushed out of the lungs rather than shouted.
Wouldn't your voice fail? Imagine advancing

with an empty musket through geysers of dirt,
trying to control your voice and your fear.
Wouldn't your legs fail…

while cannon loaded with canister and grape,
with chain and explosive shells,
blew your comrades into a bloody mist?

Chances are
1862-1863

you're learning that your horsemanship
    will count for little or nothing
you may get there first
    but get killed faster
Chances are when you do fight
    you'll be badly hurt as the killing power
of new weapons reaches
    new heights of efficiency
and if you stay back the bivouac is so rough
    chances are you'll get sick
so sick you won't get well
    typhoid   dysentery   pneumonia
make your choice
    Chances are you'll get by with a certain
native toughness
    a sardonic humour by the time
no one talks about *the cause* anymore
    but night will be the sorriest time
when you know you're getting the worst of it
    Chances are that even you, an officer
a Southern gentleman
    will join in the sad songs
tenting tonight on the old campground
    the mouth organ wailing *Lorena*
a jilted parson's lament
    The sun can never dip so low
    a-down affection's cloudless sky.
Chances are

Honest Abe and the Myth Kitty

It was not until The Emancipation Proclamation (January 1863)
that Abraham Lincoln publicly rejected his views that freed
slaves should 'voluntarily' be 'colonised 'elsewhere.'

His big lawyer ears, long-lobed,
listening for the tune of the times.

His jaw, cutting-edge sincere with
its dark fringe of patriarchal beard.

Shopkeeper, who if he short-
changed a customer by pennies

would close his store to hand-deliver
the correct change no matter how far

he had to walk: *a monomaniac*
for honesty, according to his wife;

his too-young death
from Booth's single bullet,

the perfect way to go down in history
as a good man, an orator:

conceived in liberty and dedicated
to the proposition that all men
are created equal...

He forgot to say that those slaves
newly freed, would be offered

a separate equality, away from a white
America, invited to volunteer

to board ships again -- sailing somewhere else
to be black and free.

'Ivanhoe': His Boy's Own War

*The **Ivanhoe** was an iron-hulled paddle-wheel steam ship,*
designed to evade the blockading Union fleet.

On June 5, 1864, my great-grandfather describes
something of an excitement in the shape
of 'a small misunderstanding' with our Yankee friends
about a little English boat,
how the guns of the enemy awakened them
about midnight, like the harsh rolling
of an alarming drum,

then all to their respective batteries
in a high state of rage and patriotism –
eager to pour our volleyed thunder'
on the vandal foe, a phrase he quotes
from the late newspaper. He jokes

There was an hour in which many a blood-thirsty
mosquito was sent to that country
from whose borders no mosquito
*was ever known to return...*then reports a to-ing
and fro-ing of engagements – five gunboats,
a sloop of war, a skirmish in which the Ivanhoe
retaliated, pouring in a hot fire of shot and shell,
heavy and light, round and cylindrical.
and he, remaining on guard until breakfast,
his return (this in his casual voice, *'diversified'*
by falling shot, bursting shell.

But in the end, in this toy war, nobody
was hurt, and his sole regret, he writes, is
that some of my men behaved badly –
I will have to prefer charges against them.

The First Time my Great-grandfather
Mentions Black People
May 18, 1864

It is page 63 of his letters, a Southern gentleman,
to his future wife, before the word *negro* comes up,
though he's been surrounded by black servants all his life:

nannies, cooks, housemaids, livery boys. They have sung to him,
scolded him, dressed and undressed him, pampered him,
but here, a young soldier gazing at a miniature of
my future great-grandmother, he records the exchange:

> 'a *negro* boy' had entered the room and was making up
> the bed
> behind where I am sitting:
> *Where you get dat pretty, Lieutenant Tarleton?*
> *Dat what,* replied I, *Dat lady der*
> *Is dat your sweetheart?*

My great-grandfather tells a lie, says you are his sister, Miss Sallie,
adds that *stories are sometimes necessary.* Says he thought
this *Ethiopian* might come from Demopolis, the town
where your family lives, and his carelessness might be *discovered*

that a photo seen by a black youth might bring disgrace?
A lover's fantasy, I wonder. Or a very bad joke.

Corn Bread Straight

June 16, 1864

To be sick anywhere is bad enough, he writes,
to one of his *'impatient'* disposition, *but to be sick
at Fort Morgan is surely the worst except
for the release from the senseless round of drilling.*
Now, alas he can report himself *fit for duty.*

But his mess, it seems has been on the point
of starvation, or rather reduced to the paltry diet
of 'corn bread straight,' and try as I might
I can find no recipe for this despised ingredient
of my poor great-grandfather's diet that year.

The stress is on the 'straight', and I'm thinking
coarse corn meal and whatever water is available,
guessing at the absence of eggs, of fresh milk,
of butter to alleviate its tongue-trapping dryness,
and baked in a smudgy oven or griddled
on a blackened skillet, tacky with the stale
crumbs of the last griddling.

Every day they sit down to a board which does not
groan, and some facetious party, he cites Ferguson,
who, as if at his wit's end for a remedy to their misery,
breaks out with: *Well, I move we appoint some member
of the mess to get married and invite his wife down here to do
for us, and for some reason this is always directed at me.*

I imagine my great-grandfather summoning his bride-to-be,
imagine her arriving at the door of his mess with a wicker basket,
a white linen cloth to cover, cape across her shoulders, a rebel
Red Riding Hood ready to feed those ravenous lupine officers.

Furlough

July 19, 1864, Fort Morgan

He writes: *Because they propose to cut down*
the citadel, that tall decagonal structure
in the centre of the fort –

to make it several feet off the ground
to bomb-proof it -- there's no furlough.
They're saying the Yanks are near

Tuskegee, which, though six or seven miles
from the railroad, is that kind of place
no one ever gets to unless he starts

to go there and nowhere else, with nothing
to tempt even a Yankee raider –
still no furlough

and he is so anxious to see her
and looks forward to the fall,
an impatience that makes time creep

like a snail, and he thinks he might get a furlough
to go to China and return, before Fort Morgan
or Mobile is seriously attacked –

no furlough, no furlough, no furlough.
He scratches desperation onto hoarded paper
in his youthful irrational heart's blood:

You know I am not my own man now,
but Sally, Sally, shilly shally Sally,
why won't you name the day?

360 Miles

5 August 1864, the fall of Fort Morgan

Stinking hot and sticky in August, he'd have been footsore,
thirsty, itching on the journey from Alabama to New Orleans,
my great-grandfather taken prisoner by the Yankees

after the fall of Fort Morgan. Soldiers were not famed for kindness
toward captured foe. His mind would've been turning to family,
huddled in waiting, his fiancée craving news, dreading

what she might hear; his last act, burning all her letters, hoping
to protect her. The Arsenal, then a makeshift Yankee prison,
still faces St Peter Street in the French quarter, a prime example

of Greek Revival style. Painted white, symmetrical in shape,
with pilasters, columns – everyday antebellum, unimposing for
a Southern Gentleman, a young officer trained in gymnastics: fighter,

doctor, skilled with his hands, thinking how easy to get a friend
to bring him a saw to cut a hole through such a ceiling.
He'd have gauged the proximity of roofs, alleys, fortification

of windows, doors. Not a word appears in his letters home
of what he endured trudging back over the 360 miles that starts
by crossing a chunk of Louisiana, a state you can't leave without

running into bayou to be raked by low branches of cypress, swamped
by dank curtains of Spanish moss, accosted by alligators.
Not written down, but murmured and whispered into the warm dark

from the safety of my great-grandmother's embrace: his legacy,
her recurring dream of him returning again and again
from prison, older and more wasted each time, when she'd run

to him, clutching his skeletal arms, pulling at his ragged, filthy
clothing, pulling and pulling him back from a hell she'd have
guessed at even if he'd not told her all the wretchedness.

40 Acres and a Mule

*The institution of slavery is a stain on this nation's soul that will never be
cleansed...a huge sin. There's a second sin that's almost as great and
that's emancipation.*

(Shelby Foote, 'The Atlantic Monthly, 13 June 2011)

And it came to pass that as the Union armies
advanced through the vanquished South,
thousands of slaves were freed each day;

each and every one told: *You are free, hit the road:*
three-quarters unable to read or write, not one tenth
with a profession, bar farming – turned loose.

In Caddo Parish, 1865, my great-grandfather writes that
*the Negroes believe themselves entitled to land
and stock and crops, 40 acres and a mule, that they say
will be divided among them by Christmas.
The Yankee soldiers tell them this.*

He hints at *dangerous consequences,* notes that
slavery had many evils, but how whites or blacks
are to live under the new regime he cannot see.

And it came to pass that though possessed of
foresight, my broken, baffled great-grandfather
would not live to witness what happened
when the Union Army withdrew after
a dozen years of occupation: lynch mobs
swaggering in to take control, burning crosses,
the order of the noose.

The Second Time my Great-grandfather Mentions Black People
January 1867

De-mobbed and demoralised, my great-grandfather
writes to his wife of his fears for their future,

apologises that he has *nothing of interest to write about,'*
bemoans the fact that he cannot hire 'hands' to till

the land he's kept and must cultivate in order to support
his little family in the new world of emancipation. Not ever

a hands-on farmer, he writes that when he returns to Alabama,
it will not be to plant, that he is *sick enough of the business*

and what follows is hard for me to read:

I am so tired of talking and thinking about free niggers
that I wish I was able to go to some country where
the creatures were never heard of. Go where you will here,
the talk is of the everlasting Sambo.

I think I hear the furious scratch of his pen as he dips
it in and out of an inkwell, but guessing

he might have been an owner of a recently patented
fountain pen. I am trying to forgive him

for words politely excised from common parlance 2020,
words in everyday use in the post-war misery of 1867,

and to see him as a loving father, a decent gentleman
fallen on hard times, using that vocabulary.

Misery and the falling away of nobility? He misses
his wife; complains of her long absence visiting family

and friends elsewhere, suggests that *when he gets used to
her being away from him, he may get along better.*

My Great-grandmother as Scarlett O'Hara

i.m. Sallie Lightfoot Tarleton (1821 – 1898) 'My mother's brief romance ended so soon with the death of her husband, and the difficulties of establishing herself in a world overwhelmed with poverty and uncertainties...a beautiful woman who could have married again...'

Sarah Tarleton Colvin, 'A Rebel in Thought' Island Press, 1944

I try to imagine you at Tara, Sallie Lightfoot,
on your knees in a field of turnips (or was it
potatoes?), like Vivien Leigh playing Scarlett,
raging against Sherman's evil work,
vowing never to go hungry again:
hair wild, your unaccustomed apron
grimy with grease and blood – kitchen dirt.

So much behind you: music, dancing,
fine wine, spirited horses, good books,
gentleman callers on the front veranda,
you, catching my great-grandfather's eye:
young Robert Tarleton, just down
from Princeton, plunged head first into
the politics of secession, ready to fight
for his land, your land, the glory--

your way of life, already receding.
And though the turnips were real enough,
the hunger, the poverty (your bridesmaids
in homespun muslin, hand-woven
on the plantation, your wedding gown
passed down through sisters and cousin-brides),
my Tara image slips away to a sorrowing woman,
early widowed, who never put on colours

after mourning for her husband,
for the genteel past, the South you knew
and loved, who near your death on a 4th of July,
railed at the nurse who brought in
a small American flag
your voice strong as ever:
Take that flag out of this room.

R.I.P.

Robert Melvin Tarleton,
born: 20 June 1838,
died: 28 September 1868

My great-grandfather,
only 30 years old:

Had imprisonment
compromised his health?

I read from his obituary:

Enlisted as a private and as such,
saw some rough times:

escaped from a Yankee prison
waded armpit deep

through swamps around New Orleans
to come in time to marry Sallie Lightfoot.

The deceased leaves three children:
two daughters, Sarah and Margaret,

born on the evening of the day of his death,
and a son, Robert Melvin Tarleton Jr.

His death resulted from congestion of
the bowels, a happy death, surrounded
by his family. So ends the human life,

writes the author,

and so begins the glorious immortality
of one of the very noblest of men.

And who, now or then, will have
the audacity to judge him? Not I.

ii. The Cause

I look at the stand of trees near the bayou
and instead of a tractor engine idling there
I hear the popping of small-arms fire,
see black plumes of smoke exploding
out of the brush into the sunlight,
and I'm imagining that they died, those boys,
right here in this field, that they bled
into this same dirt where cane
would grow eight feet tall by autumn,
and turn it russet as dried blood.

Epitaph 2020
after my cousin, Ippy Patterson

Too little has changed, you write
describing how you tried to break
some cotton off close to the root
in a field in the dark a few weeks
before Christmas, but found it
impossible.
The branch would bend,
but not break. Grabbing
an old pocket-knife in your car,
you tried again, though nervous
at being parked on the side
of a country road in the South,
your South now, at midnight,
and sliced through part
of a fingernail, drove home
sucking that bleeding finger
feeling you had stolen something
and that you were right
to cut yourself in the process,
feeling that you,
or any of us
could ever know
the whisper
of the pain inflicted
in that troubled time,
and suffered from still.

NOTES:

Myth Kitty: A body of myths, which may be stories known and re-told, but known and shared by the members of a particular community or belief system.

Antebellum 'before the war,' not widely associated with the U.S. Civil War until after the conflict was over.

Cold Mountain, a 1997 historical novel by Charles Frazier which won the U.S. National Book Award for Fiction

The Civil War, by Bruce Catton, American Heritage Books, first published 1961-1963

Rebel in Thought, by Sarah Tarleton Colvin, Island Press, 1944.